I would like to thank those who helped me with this project:

Nell Casto who proofed this book, as well as my first book on growing up in Kilmarnock, VA.

My daughter Tara for the design and post production work.

My wife Lynn who continually reads, re-reads and gives me honest input on my writings.

Anna Leigh Davis and family for reading the book before being published.

This book is dedicated to the men and women who go out of their
way to protect the lives of animals.

It is written in a fashion to be read to a child, by a child, or shared as a
gift to anyone who loves animals and, especially in this case, cats.

* Due to the fact that some images of Tiny were taken randomly with a
cell phone they may not be of the highest quality.

Tiny is the name that our family gave to a little black and white ball of fur that came to our house accompanied by his mother. The first time we saw Tiny was when his mother decided we were a good family with a safe place for him to take up residence. His little legs were so new he could hardly sit up!

His mother, "Platinum", came every day and night to eat food we fixed for her and a few other cats that didn't seem to have homes. Cats that don't have homes are afraid of people, so we decided that Tiny was going to be different.

We were going to seek a two way love from Tiny, plus confidence and trust.

On our carport we immediately fixed a nice warm bed under a table, draped a quilt down the sides of the table, and supplied a low wattage bulb to create some heat. After all, it was March and very cold, and Tiny was still depending on his mother for food.

Tiny's mother seemed very pleased that her few weeks old kitten was getting such good treatment and she didn't mind our picking up Tiny. In fact she seemed to enjoy Tiny being loved, and she trusted us totally.

Tiny spent most of his time under the table in his newly created home, but once in a while we could see him peek out from under the quilt to see what was on the other side of his world. It was so much fun to see something so little trying to learn to be like the other cats that were much larger.

Tiny was accepted by everyone, which was a good thing since Platinum made sure that any of the other cats that came along treated Tiny well! Once or twice, Platinum had to correct them with a gentle tap of her paw. They soon learned that Tiny had full authority to go up to any of them without fear of being pushed away.

Each day Tiny grew stronger and slightly larger and gained more confidence to be like the other cats in his adopted family. Those first few weeks were a bonding and teaching experience provided by his brave and proud mother.

As time went on, Tiny learned to eat dry food just like the other cats, though at times he had to improvise because everything in his world seemed much larger and harder to get to than for the other cats.

It wasn't long before Tiny would line up like the rest of the cats and eat at the same time. He felt so big and brave doing this, and he loved every minute of it!

As soon as Tiny was old enough, we took him to the veterinarian to be checked over and given his proper shots to make sure he was in good health and would stay that way.

Tiny had his first ride in a car to go to the doctor, and soon we were inside where he patiently waited his turn to see the doctor.

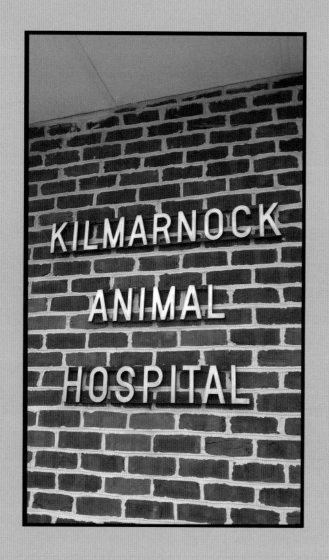

When it was Tiny's turn, the assistant called his name and took him to the table where he was weighed, checked out and given his shots. It was almost as if he knew what was coming and was prepared to leave before seeing the doctor.

It was time for Tiny to have his own bed on "TOP" of the table, not on the bottom where he had to peek out to see what was going on. He really enjoyed having a top bunk and being able to look all around.

Tiny loved to be played with while in his top bunk, and he felt very safe having a lamp that kept him warm at night.

As the days and weeks moved on, Tiny was old enough to love toys. He loved the scratching toy that he played on and under and knew was his!

Tiny could make a game out of anything. He just loved where he lived and all the attention he was getting. He knew he had a home and people who loved him, and <u>that</u> we did!

Close to Tiny's bed and table was a mirror that leaned up against the wall and somehow Tiny found his way to the mirror to get a firsthand look at himself. I don't think he was sure at first if it was he or another cat, but he sat for a while and tried to make up his mind.

Before you knew it, Tiny was big enough to explore the yard, but only if his mom Platinum was right by his side or very close by. She remained protective of him and taught him caution and all the tricks she knew for getting away from trouble.

I looked one day and Tiny was learning how to climb a tree! Sometimes Tiny would climb up a little ways then his mom would go up just behind him to make sure he knew he was safe, but the instructions always started at the bottom of the tree.

From that day on, Tiny always knew to stay in the yard, but to travel to all parts of it to become familiar with his surroundings. Just as you can see, Tiny was everywhere checking out every place in the yard he could, and, most of the time, Platinum was close by for added protection.

After that we found Tiny finding a bed to rest in, most anywhere. We never knew from day to day where Tiny would decide to take a nap, but one thing was for sure, he was close by.

One day Tiny decided that an empty birdbath would make a wonderful resting place for the afternoon.

We could almost see him saying "Please don't move me from here; it's the best spot I have found all day"!

One of Tiny's most favorite places to rest during the day was in a cat bed on the table of the patio. He loved this spot during the day and many nights when warm.

One day I called and called Tiny, but he just wasn't around, or it seemed. I decided to look out in the front yard to see if he had wandered there.

I could almost feel Tiny looking at me, or that he was very near, but I just didn't see him. Tiny never ran off, so I knew he was somewhere close.

Just then I noticed something that just didn't belong in the flower box under the window of our home. Yes, it was Tiny who had found a nice comfy place that felt good.

We loved to see Tiny enjoy his home, and we wanted him to find good, safe places to lie since cats sleep a lot!

Written all over his face was: "Please don't even think about moving me. We didn't!

Tiny could make a game out of anything. Whether it was in the yard, or with a toy in his bed, Tiny loved to have fun.

Tiny was having a lot of fun but he wasn't the only one; we were as well. We had taken a little life that needed a home, love and attention, and, in return, we were getting the same things.

Tiny made friends with any animals that were in the yard. He made the first effort by rolling over in front of them and seeking friendship. He knew how to make friends just as he is shown here meeting his new friend Westbrook.

Tiny is almost as large as the other cats now and he loves to come up to meet us, walk in the house and look around, or play outside all day and night.

Even though Tiny is older, Platinum is still around to protect him if it's needed. Just as we have parents, cats do too, and they want to make sure their children are well trained, protected and loved.

Now that Tiny has grown up a lot, I think he knows that having his picture taken is a very normal thing and we can look back when he was little, growing fast, or now when he is "Tiny" the Cat!

There are lots of beautiful cats, just like Tiny, that need a home; a home that can give two-way love, just as we have developed with Tiny.

They don't require a lot to live, they just need to be fed, have their shots and other medical attention, a warm place to sleep in the winter, and a person who wants plenty of love in return.

Cats depend on people to provide them with a quality life. One of the greatest acts of love anyone could ever consider is adopting a kitten and training it to be confident of love before it gets too old.

If the reader doesn't know where to look for a kitten, contact an Animal Welfare League or an S.P.C.A. These organizations can point anyone in the direction of a kitten needing love and ready to return that love to its owner.